LEONARDO DA VINCI

ARTIST, INVENTOR AND SCIENTIST

ART HISTORY LESSONS FOR KIDS

Children's Art Books

BABY PROFESSOR
EDUCATION KIDS

Speedy Publishing LLC
40 E. Main St. #1156
Newark, DE 19711
www.speedypublishing.com

n this book, we're going to talk about the life of Leonardo da Vinci. So, let's get right to it!

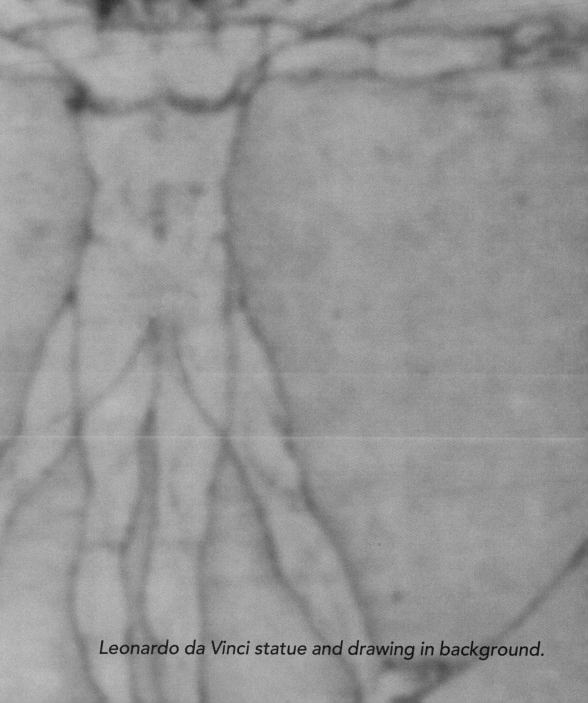

Leonardo da Vinci statue and drawing in background.

WHO WAS LEONARDO DA VINCI?

It's difficult to classify Leonardo da Vinci. He was an artist who excelled in painting, sculpting, and architectural design, but he was also a scientist and an inventor. He was forever studying and learning because he had a naturally curious mind. His painting masterpieces and his visionary ideas from the High Renaissance period in Italy have inspired artists and scientists throughout the centuries.

LEONARDO'S EARLY LIFE

The rural area of Anchiano in Tuscany, Italy was Leonardo's birthplace in 1452 AD. His father was a respected notary from the city of Florence and his mother Caterina was a peasant girl who wasn't married to his father. He was raised by his father, Ser Piero, and stepmothers.

Leonardo da Vinci.

When Leonardo was five years old, he moved to the Tuscan town of Vinci, which became his surname. There, at his father's estate, he lived with his uncle and his grandparents.

Leonardo da Vinci.

Leonardo didn't have much formal education. He learned to read and write and received some instruction in mathematics. Very early on, his amazing talent for art was evident. His father noticed and encouraged him.

Study of horses by Leonardo Da Vinci.

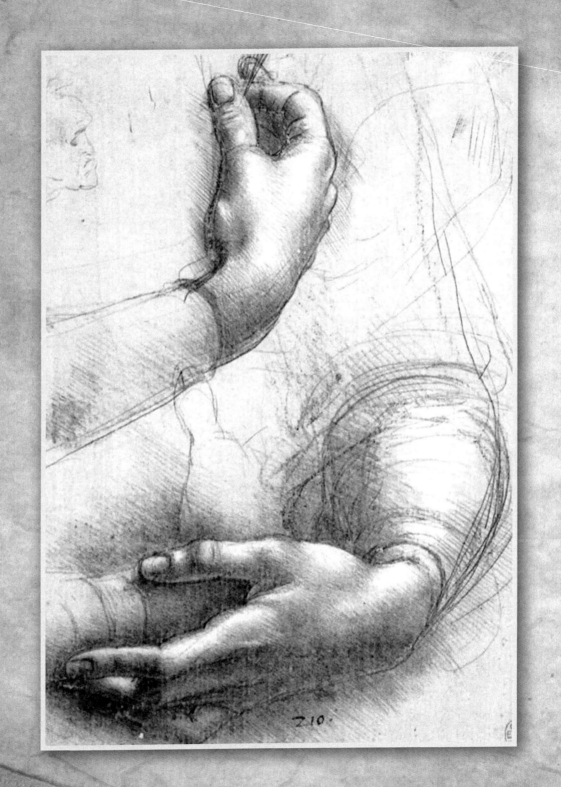

When Leonardo was 14 years old, his father sent him to work with the famous artist Andrea del Verrocchio who had a studio in Florence. Leonardo became Verrocchio's apprentice and learned his trade during the twelve years he was there.

Study of hands by Leonardo Da Vinci.

Leonardo mastered painting and sculpting while working with Verrocchio, but he also mastered creating with metal, carpentry, and creating objects with leather. His first dated work was a drawing of the beautiful Arno valley done in pen and ink in 1473 AD. Leonardo graduated from Verrocchio's apprenticeship and was ready to go out as an independent artist in 1478.

Head of an Old Man by Leonardo Da Vinci.

"Annunciation" by Leonardo da Vinci.

MOVING TO MILAN

The Medici Family had been powerful bankers and eventually rulers in Italy since the 13th century. In 1482, Lorenzo de' Medici, who was the ruler of Florence, gave Leonardo a commission. He wanted Leonardo to construct a special silver lyre, which is a musical instrument with strings similar to a harp. This lyre was important because it would be presented to Ludovico Sforza who was the ruler of the powerful city-state of Milan.

Leonardo created the beautiful lyre and he saw an opportunity. After he presented the lyre to Ludovico, Leonardo returned home, but he sent Ludovico a letter stating that he was looking for a job and describing his talents as a military engineer.

Vitruvian Man.

Leonardo sketched war machines that were ahead of their time such as war chariots with blades mounted on each side. Another sketch showed an armored tank that was operated by two soldiers turning a shaft.

He even had a sketch of a huge crossbow that would have taken a small army to operate. Leonardo's imaginative drawings accomplished his goal. Ludovico Sforza hired him and Leonardo traveled to Milan and worked for the Sforza family for 17 years.

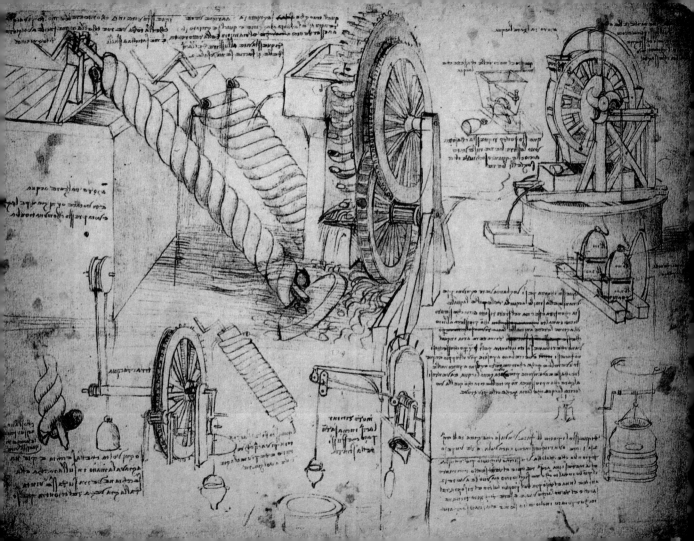

During his work for the Sforza family, Leonardo advised them on military engineering as well as architectural design. He also created masterpieces in the form of paintings and sculptures. He had a thirst for knowledge in a huge range of subjects. Leonardo was a humanist and at this time the humanist movement was becoming an important belief system during the Renaissance.

Leonardo da Vinci's old engineering drawing.

Humanism encouraged people to think that life could be enjoyable. Their lives should be filled with beautiful experiences with art and music. For humanists, there wasn't a division between art and science. Instead, Leonardo believed that from studying the science of human anatomy he could become a better artist.

Leonardo da Vinci's old engineering drawing.

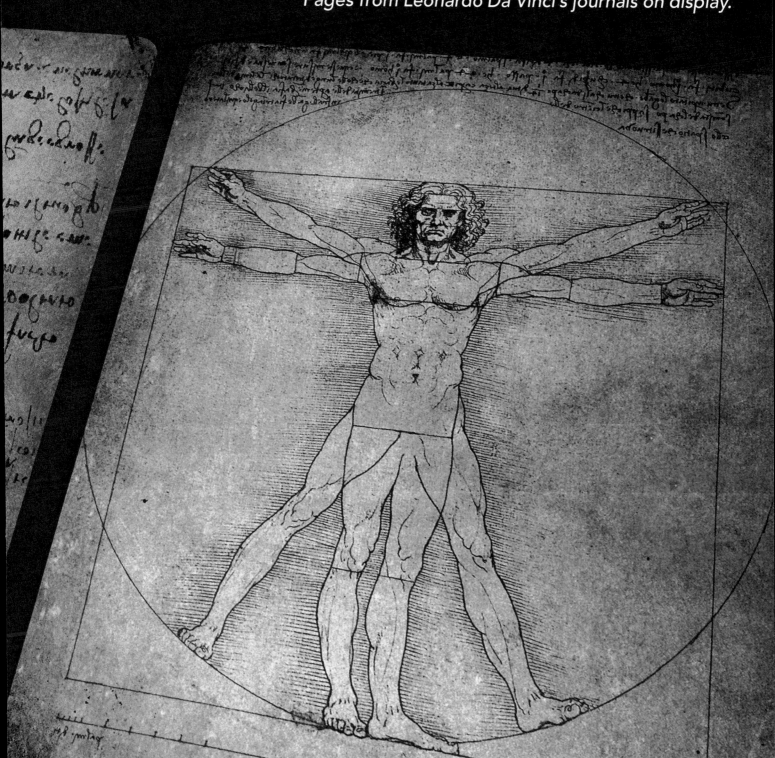
Pages from Leonardo Da Vinci's journals on display.

LEONARDO'S NOTEBOOKS

In addition to the human anatomy, Leonardo studied botany, zoology, and geology. He dissected dead bodies to find out more about anatomy and filled his notebooks with sketches. He was fascinated by hydraulics and physics. He sketched many visionary inventions including flying machines that were 300 years ahead of their time. In his notebooks he used mirror writing. You couldn't read what he had written unless you looked at his page of handwriting in a mirror.

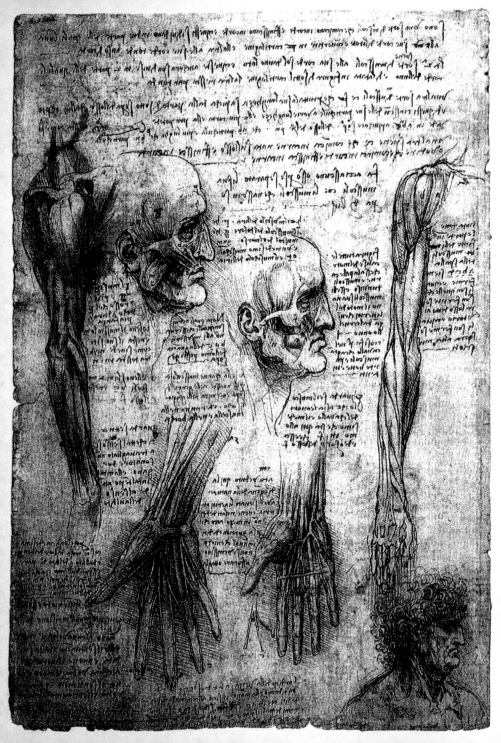

No one knows precisely why Leonardo did this. He was left-handed so it could have been because he didn't want the ink to smear as he was writing. Another possible reason is that he didn't want his journals to be read by the Catholic Church if they were found. After all, it was illegal for Leonardo to be performing dissections because he wasn't formally trained as a doctor. In any case, his mirror writing was a way of cleverly disguising his work.

Pages from Leonardo Da Vinci's journals on display.

Leonardo's journals were filled with his ideas and detailed scientific observations. He arranged the subjects of his notes into four very broad themes—painting, human anatomy, mechanics, and architecture.

Pages from Leonardo Da Vinci's journals on display.

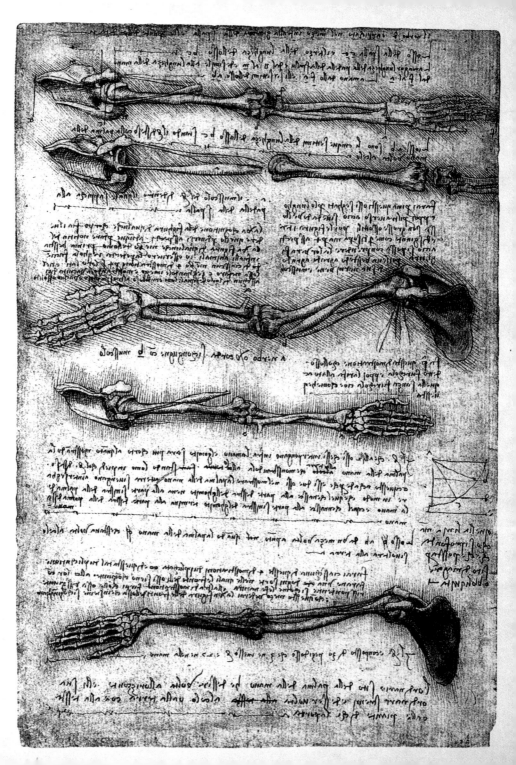

Today, about 7,000 pages of his notebooks have survived. In 1994, the billionaire Bill Gates bought one of Leonardo's notebooks called the Codex Leicester for $30.8 million dollars.

Pages from Leonardo Da Vinci's journals on display.

Restored "The Last Supper" by Leonardo da Vinci.

THE LAST SUPPER

In 1495, Ludovico hired Leonardo to do a painting depicting the scene in the New Testament when Christ has the last supper with his Twelve Apostles before he is betrayed and then crucified. The painting was to be created on the back wall of the dining room in the convent of Santa Maria delle Grazie where the Dominican nuns would gather for their meals.

The size of the final painting was to be 15 feet tall by 29 feet wide. In order to get the perspective in the painting correct, Leonardo hammered a nail into the wall and drew lines out from it to ensure that the depth would be correct. Every face in the painting was modeled after a real person. Legend has it that Leonardo based the model for the face of Judas on the face of a criminal he found in Milan's jail.

The painting captured the dramatic moment over Passover dinner when Jesus told them that one of them would betray him soon. The expressions on the figures in the painting as well as the body language and positioning brought the painting to life.

Leonardo had a reputation for procrastinating, which simply means that he was slow to begin projects, worked slowly when he started, and was easily distracted. He decided not to use the standard fresco method of painting on wet plaster because he would have to work too fast. Also, the fresco method wouldn't give the painting the feeling of light he wanted to show.

Heads of Judas and Peter from Leonardo da Vinci's "The Last Supper".

He decided to use a method that used tempera paint and oil paint on dried plaster. Unfortunately, even geniuses can make mistakes. Over time, *"The Last Supper"* began to flake off the walls. In recent years, the painting has been completely restored although not much of the original paint remains.

Part of Leonardo da Vinci's "The Last Supper".

Mona Lisa - detail of smile.

THE MONA LISA

After a period of time, Leonardo went back to Florence. Beginning in 1502, he had a position as Cesare Borgia's military engineer. Cesare was the head of the pope's army. Leonardo traveled out of the city to survey projects in construction. He sketched city plans as well as topographical maps. He also designed plans to change the path of the Arno River so that Florence's enemy, the city of Pisa, couldn't get access to the sea.

Next, Leonardo was commissioned to do a painting of the *"Battle of Anghiari."* It was a wall that was twice as large as that of the Last Supper. After two years, he gave up on the project because it had already started to decay. At the same time, Leonardo began work on what eventually became his most famous painting—the Mona Lisa. It's believed that this painting, which was painted on a wood panel, was commissioned and that it was a portrait of Lisa del Gioconda, who was a wealthy silk merchant's wife.

However, this information isn't known with 100% certainty. If it wasn't her, than there are many theories of who might have been the model for the portrait. Leonardo used a special painting technique called **sfumato**, which blends tones and colors gradually producing a soft look.

Whoever commissioned the painting never received it. Perhaps Leonardo recognized that it was the peak of his talent. He couldn't part with it. The lady with the mysterious smile was by his bedside when he died. The painting was willed to one of Leonardo's students and eventually sold to the King of France for 4,000 gold coins. Today, the Mona Lisa is known worldwide and it shown, behind bulletproof glass, to millions of people every year in the Louvre museum in Paris. Recent estimates state that the painting is worth at least $1 billion dollars.

"Mona Lisa" by Leonardo da Vinci.

Unlike other Renaissance painters like Raphael who painted hundreds of paintings in his lifetime, Leonardo only painted a few paintings during his life, but they are all considered masterpieces.

A copy of "Mona Lisa" by an apprentice of Leonardo da Vinci.

Over the centuries, thousands of pages of his private journals have surfaced which show the measure of his genius. Today, we call someone who has interests and talents in both the arts and sciences, a Renaissance man or woman after this first true Renaissance man.

Awesome! Now you know more about the amazing life and achievements of Leonardo da Vinci. You can find more Art books from Baby Professor by searching the website of your favorite book retailer.

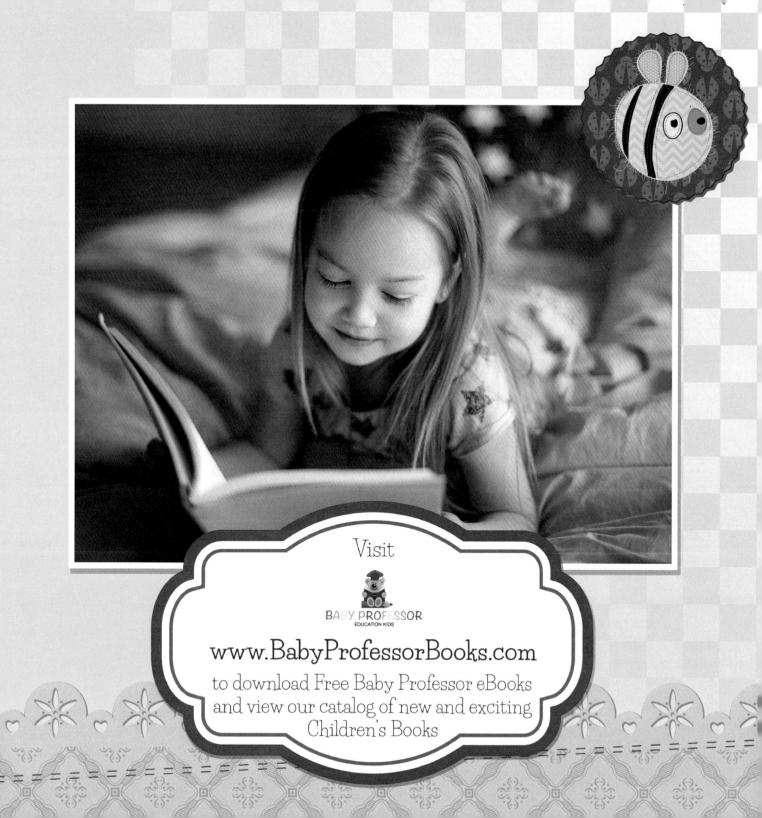

Visit

BABY PROFESSOR
EDUCATION KIDS

www.BabyProfessorBooks.com

to download Free Baby Professor eBooks
and view our catalog of new and exciting
Children's Books

Made in United States
North Haven, CT
10 December 2021

12449372R00038